… *the dots are small and easy to make.*

And, as I add more and more,

they gradually cover the canvas

and join together to form a beautiful picture."

big & SMALL

Original Korean text by In-sook Kim
Illustrations by Se-yeon Jeong
Korean edition © Aram Publishing

This English edition published by big & SMALL in 2017
by arrangement with Aram Publishing
English text edited by Scott Forbes
English edition © big & SMALL 2017

Distributed in the United States and Canada by
Lerner Publishing Group, Inc.
241 First Avenue North
Minneapolis, MN 55401 U.S.A.
www.lernerbooks.com

ISBN: 978-1-925235-29-6

Printed in Korea

Joining the Dots

THE ART OF SEURAT

Written by In-sook Kim
Illustrated by Se-yeon Jeong
Edited by Scott Forbes

For a long time the artist had been wondering: Could he paint colors in a different way? Could he show how they blended together in nature and changed in bright light and shade?

Every day he went to the park to watch the sun glittering on the river and the shadows of the trees moving across the grass. He observed the people around him and how their shapes and colors changed when they were far away.

One day, the artist decided to paint a picture in a different way.

First, he dipped the tip of his brush into some paint and touched it lightly on the canvas.

8

9

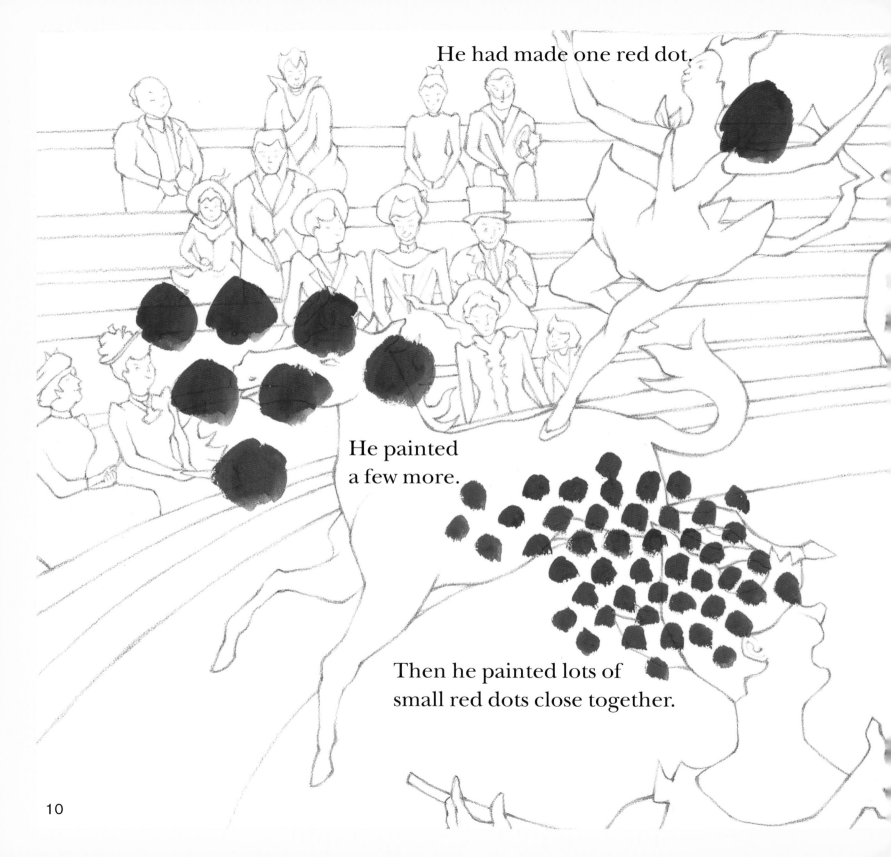

He had made one red dot.

He painted
a few more.

Then he painted lots of
small red dots close together.

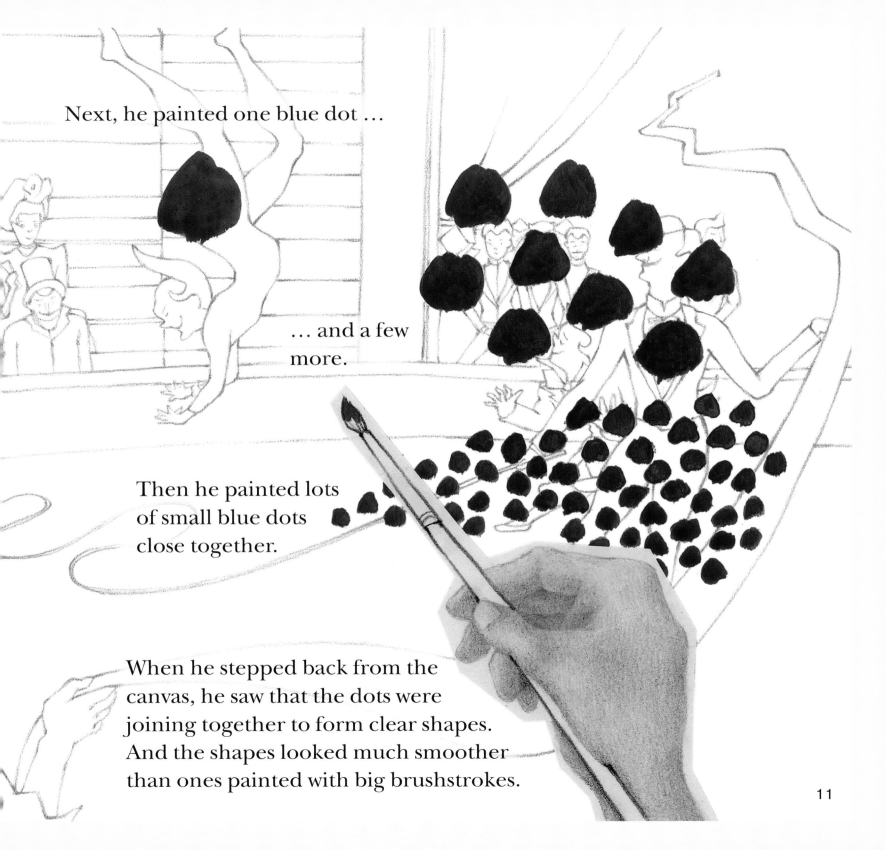

Next, he painted one blue dot …

… and a few more.

Then he painted lots of small blue dots close together.

When he stepped back from the canvas, he saw that the dots were joining together to form clear shapes. And the shapes looked much smoother than ones painted with big brushstrokes.

11

Next, he tried painting lines of dots.
He painted lines in one color, then in another color.
After that, he tried mixing different-colored dots.

"Aha!" he said.
"That's it!"

The Circus (1890–91), Musée d'Orsay, Paris, France

The artist realized that by mixing dots of different colors, he could create another color. For example, blue dots mixed with red dots created purple.

14

If he added more red dots than blue dots, he made a deep reddish purple, like crimson. And, if he mixed more blue dots and fewer red dots, he created a bluish purple, like lilac.

15

The artist began painting lots
of blue dots onto the canvas.
He painted them again and again.

16

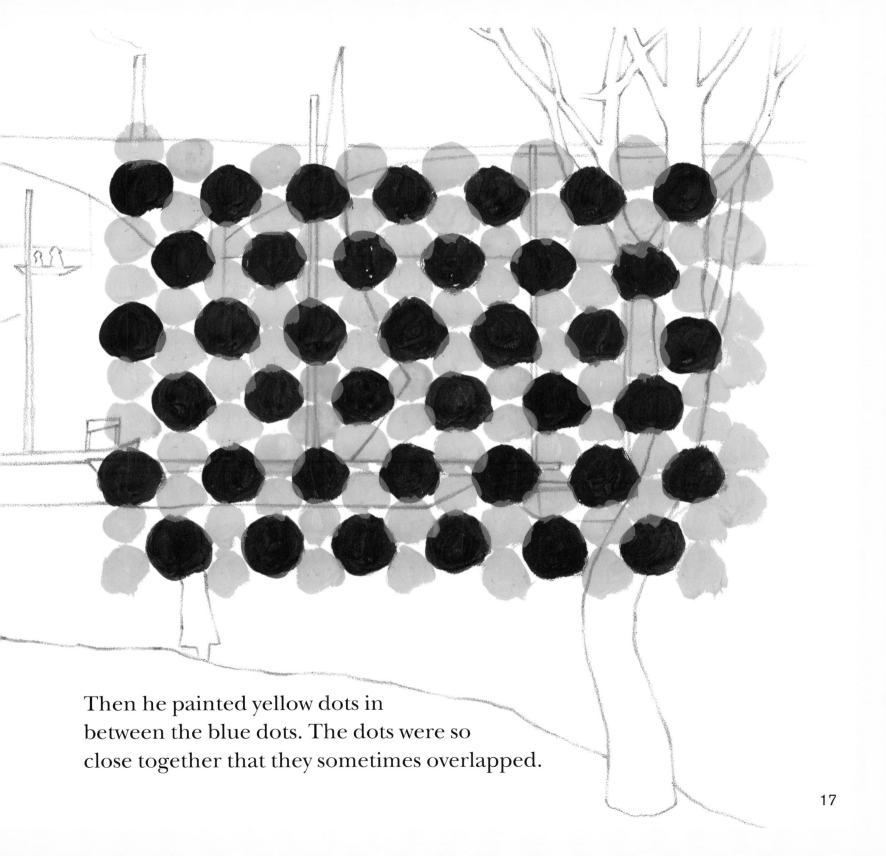

Then he painted yellow dots in
between the blue dots. The dots were so
close together that they sometimes overlapped.

17

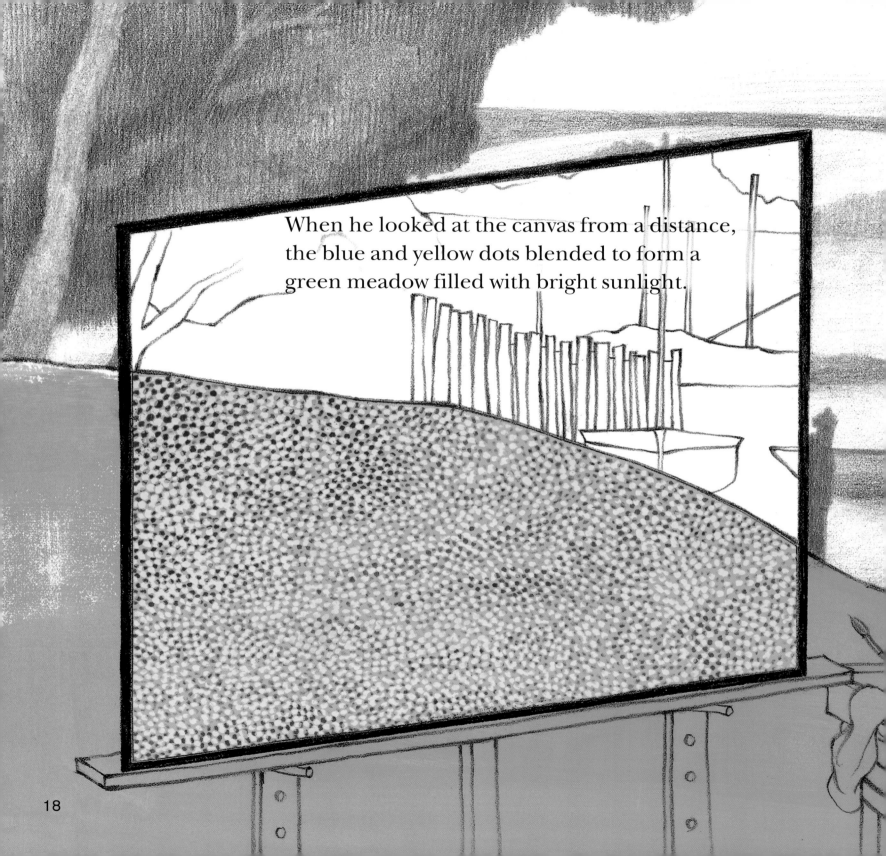

When he looked at the canvas from a distance, the blue and yellow dots blended to form a green meadow filled with bright sunlight.

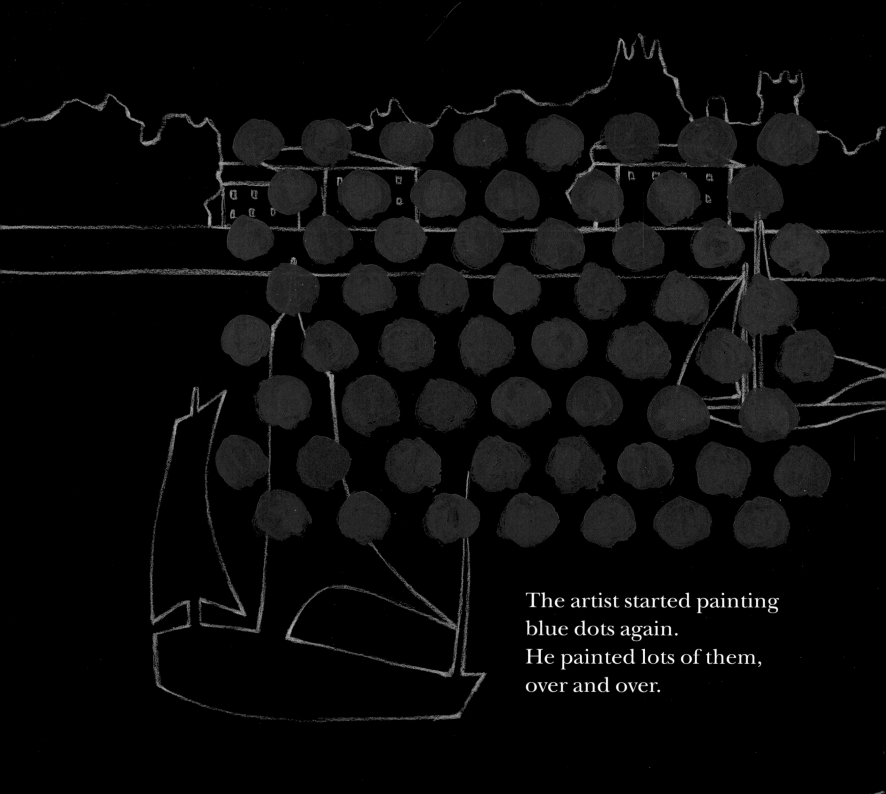

The artist started painting
blue dots again.
He painted lots of them,
over and over.

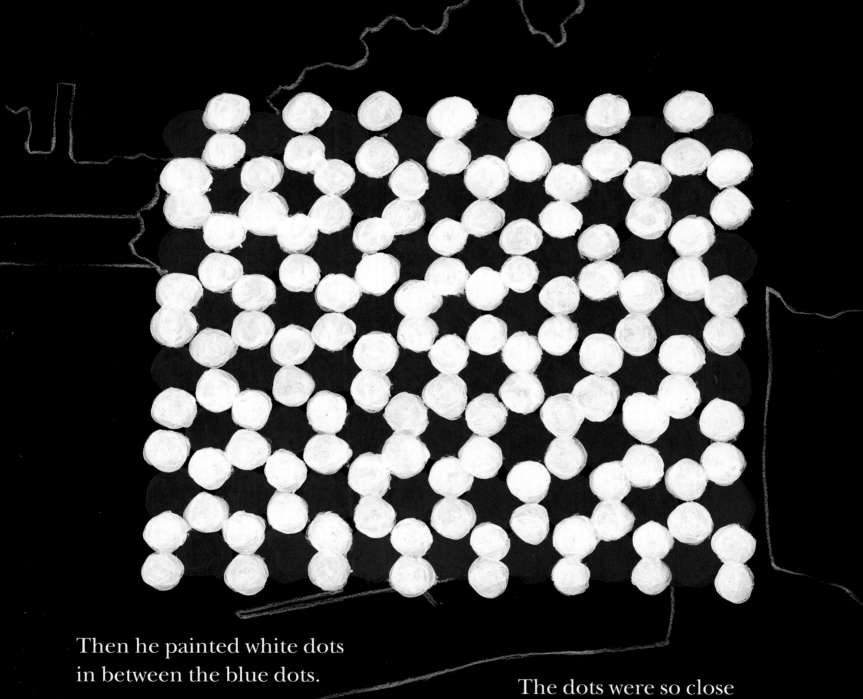

Then he painted white dots
in between the blue dots.

The dots were so close
together that they
sometimes overlapped.

Stepping back, the
artist saw a blue river
sparkling in sunlight.

23

On Sundays, lots of people
went to the park.
They enjoyed the sunshine
and bathed in the river.
They were there to relax.

Except for one person.
The artist sat quietly in the shade,
studying everything closely — the
people, the colors, the sunlight,
and the shadows.

25

He had decided to paint this scene — his favorite scene — using his new method. He had already made a drawing of the park. Now he started painting dots on it. He painted yellow dots, blue dots, and red dots. And he mixed different-colored dots to form new, marvellous colors. Slowly, the painting took shape.

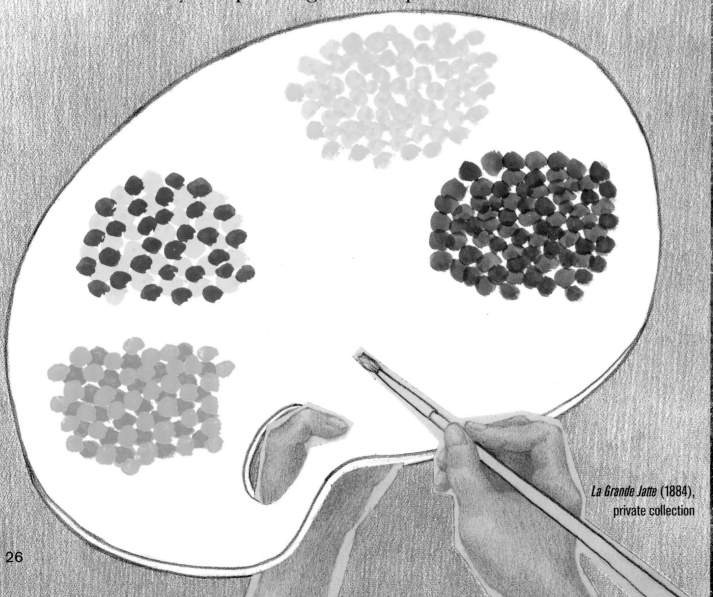

La Grande Jatte (1884), private collection

Red and yellow dots created the orange color of the clothes of the lady who is standing at the water's edge.

A Sunday on La Grande Jatte (1884), Art Institute of Chicago, Chicago, USA

Red and blue dots combined to form the dark skirt of the lady on the right in the painting.

The dots covered almost the entire painting. Only in a few places, like the white dress of this little girl, did the artist use brushstrokes instead.

Lots of dark dots blended to create the sleek coat of the dog that is sniffing the ground.

The painting was full of light, color, and life. There was so much going on in it: people walking, rowing, fishing, and eating. There was even a monkey on a leash! Did you spot it?

The painting was a magnificent display of the artist's new method. That method became known as pointillism. The artist was Georges Seurat.

A new approach to painting

As a young artist, Georges Seurat was fascinated by science. He studied the latest discoveries about how people see colors. This helped him develop a completely new style of painting.

Seeing colors

In particular, Seurat studied the works of a French chemist called Michel-Eugène Chevreul. Chevreul had noticed that if two colors are placed side by side and we view them from a distance, we see a mix of those two colors.

Seurat decided to apply this idea to painting. Traditionally, artists put blobs of different-colored paint on a palette and mixed the blobs together to make a new color. After reading Chevreul, Seurat realized that if he placed dots of different-colored paint side by side on the canvas, the eyes and brain of the viewer would do the mixing for him – and see the combined color!

So Seurat began painting with dots. He covered his canvases in thousands of dots, mixing different-colored dots to create a range of colors and effects. The smooth, rounded shapes that the dots formed also made his paintings look bold, solid, and grand. Seurat's technique became known as pointillism.

Paintings of modern life

Seurat liked to paint pictures of groups of people enjoying themselves. One of his favorite places was the island of La Grande Jatte, in the Seine River, in Paris. People went there to walk, picnic, swim, and play.

A Sunday on La Grande Jatte (1884–86), Art Institute of Chicago, Chicago, USA

This major work was Seurat's biggest painting. It is almost 7 feet (2 metres) tall and more than 10 feet (3 metres) wide.

1859
Born in Paris, France

1878
Enrols in an art school in Paris to study painting

1881
Begins experimenting with painting with dots

1884
Uses his new method to paint *Bathers at Asnières*. He submits it to France's biggest art show, the Salon, but it is rejected.

Seurat also liked to paint pictures of nightlife, such as people watching a performance in a theater or at the circus. By using larger dots in these paintings, he captured the shimmering effects of the bright lights and the performers' fancy costumes.

Tragically, Seurat died aged just 31. He left behind only 7 large paintings and about 40 small paintings. But the new method that he invented – pointillism – was soon taken up by other painters. And today Seurat's works are treasured as masterpieces of modern art.

Bathers at Asnières (1884), National Gallery, London, UK
This large painting shows a group of workers relaxing on the banks of the River Seine, in the suburb of Asnières in Paris. Before he painted works like this, Seurat made many preliminary sketches.

The Can-Can (1889–90), Kröller-Müller Museum, Otterlo, the Netherlands
The high kicks of the dancers create a striking pattern in this lively night-time painting.

The Circus (1890–91), Musée d'Orsay, Paris, France
Seurat enjoyed the exciting spectacle of the circus, with its daring performances, bright lights, and colorful costumes.

1886
Finishes his major work, *A Sunday on La Grande Jatte*

1890
Completes *The Can-Can* and is recognized as one of France's leading painters; has a son with artists' model Madeleine Knobloch

1891
Dies after a short illness on 29 March; his son dies of the same illness two weeks later